THE STOWAWAYS

Kestrel Kites is a series of lively and interesting
stories intended for beginner readers. Clear, large
print and lots of line drawings make these books ideal
for those who have just begun to enjoy reading
a complete book on their own.

Other titles in the series:

ROGER McGOUGH

THE STOWAWAYS

ILLUSTRATED BY TONY BLUNDELL

A Kestrel Kite · VIKING KESTREL

01752599

VIKING KESTREL
Penguin Books Ltd, Harmondsworth, Middlesex, England
Viking Penguin Inc., 40 West 23rd Street, New York, New York 10010, U.S.A.
Penguin Books Australia Ltd, Ringwood, Victoria, Australia
Penguin Books Canada Limited, 2801 John Street, Markham, Ontario, Canada L3R 1B4
Penguin Books (N.Z.) Ltd, 182–190 Wairau Road, Auckland 10, New Zealand

First published 1986

Text copyright © Roger McGough, 1986
Illustrations copyright © Tony Blundell, 1986

British Library Cataloguing in Publication Data

McGough, Roger
    The stowaways. —— (Viking Kestrel Kites)
    I. Title   II. Blundell, Tony
    823'.914[J]   PZ7

ISBN 0–670–80135–6

Printed in Great Britain by
Richard Clay (The Chaucer Press) Ltd, Bungay, Suffolk
Filmset by Northumberland Press Ltd, Gateshead,
Tyne and Wear

The Stowaways

When I lived in Liverpool, my best friend was a boy called Midge. Kevin Midgeley was his real name, but we called him Midge for short. And he was short, only about three cornflake packets high (empty ones at that). No three ways about it. Midge was my best friend and we had lots of things in common. Things we enjoyed doing like ... climbing trees, playing footy, going to the pictures, hitting each other really hard. And there were things we didn't enjoy doing like ... sums, washing behind our ears, eating cabbage.

But there was one thing that really bound us together, one thing we had in common — a love of the sea.

In the old days (but not so long ago) the River Mersey was far busier than it is today. Those were the days of the great passenger liners and cargo boats. Large ships sailed out of Liverpool for Canada, the United States, South Africa, the West Indies, all over the world. My father had been to sea and so had all my uncles, and my grandfather. Six foot six, muscles rippling in the wind, huge hands grappling with the helm, rum-soaked and fierce as a wounded shark (and that was only my grandmother!) By the time they were twenty, most young men in this city had visited parts of the globe I can't even spell.

In my bedroom each night, I used to lie in bed (best place to lie really), I used to lie there, especially in winter, and listen to the foghorns being sounded all down the river. I could picture the ship nosing its way out of the docks into the channel and out into the Irish Sea. It was exciting. All those exotic places. All those exciting adventures.

Midge and I knew what we wanted to do when we left school . . . become sailors. A captain, an admiral, perhaps one day even a steward. Of course we were only about seven or eight at the time so we thought we'd have a long time to wait. But oddly enough, the call of the sea came sooner than we'd expected.

It was a Wednesday if I remember rightly. I never liked Wednesdays for some reason. I could never spell it for a start and it always seemed to be raining, and there were still two days to go before the weekend. Anyway, Midge and I got into trouble at school. I don't remember what for (something trivial I suppose like chewing gum in class, forgetting how to read, setting fire to the music teacher), I forget now. But we were picked on, nagged, told off and all those boring things that grown-ups get up to sometimes.

And, of course, to make matters worse, my mum and dad were in a right mood when I got home. Nothing to do with me, of course, because as you have no doubt gathered by now, I was the perfect child: clean, well-mannered, obedient ... soft in the head. But for some reason I was clipped round the ear and sent to bed early for being childish.

Childish! I ask you. I *was* a child. A child acts his age, what does he get? Wallop!

So that night in bed, I decided ... Yes, you've guessed it. I could hear the big ships calling out to each other as they sidled out of the Mersey into the oceans beyond. The tugs leading the way like proud little guide dogs. That's it. We'd run away to sea, Midge and I. I'd tell him the good news in the morning.

The next two days just couldn't pass quickly enough for us. We had decided to begin our amazing around-the-world voyage on Saturday morning so that in case we didn't like it we would be back in time for school on Monday. As you can imagine there was a lot to think about — what clothes to take, how much food and drink. We decided on two sweaters each and wellies in case we ran into storms around Cape Horn. I read somewhere that sailors lived off rum and dry biscuits, so I poured some of my dad's into an empty pop bottle, and borrowed a handful of half-coated chocolate digestives. I also packed my lonestar cap gun and Midge settled on a magnifying glass.

On Friday night we met round at his house to make the final plans. He lived with his granny and his sister, so there were no nosy parents to discover what we were up to. We hid all the stuff in the shed in the yard and arranged to meet outside his back door next morning at the crack of dawn, or sunrise — whichever came first.

Sure enough, Saturday morning, when the big finger was on twelve and the little one was on six, Midge and I met with our little bundles under our arms and ran up the street as fast as our tiptoes could carry us.

Hardly anyone was about, and the streets were so quiet and deserted except for a few pigeons straddling home after all-night parties.

It was a very strange feeling, as if we were the only people alive and the city belonged entirely to us. And soon the world would be ours as well – once we'd stowed away on a ship bound for somewhere far off and exciting.

By the time we'd got down to the Pier Head, though, a lot more people were up and about, including a policeman who eyed us suspiciously. 'Ello, Ello, Ello,' he said, 'and where are you two going so early in the morning?'

'Fishing,' I said.

'Train spotting,' said Midge and we looked at each other.

'Just so long as you're not running away to sea.'

'Oh no,' we chorused. 'Just as if.'

He winked at us. 'Off you go then, and remember to look both ways before crossing your eyes.'

We ran off and straight down on to the landing stage where a lot of ships were tied up. There was no time to lose because already quite a few were putting out to sea, their sirens blowing, the hundreds of seagulls squeaking excitedly, all tossed into the air like giant handfuls of confetti.

Then I noticed a small ship just to the left where the crew were getting ready to cast off. They were so busy doing their work that it was easy for Midge and me to slip on board unnoticed. Up the gang-plank we went and straight up on to the top deck where there was nobody around. The sailors were all busy down below, hauling in the heavy ropes and revving up the engine that turned the great propellers.

We looked around for somewhere to hide. 'I know, let's climb down the funnel,' said Midge.

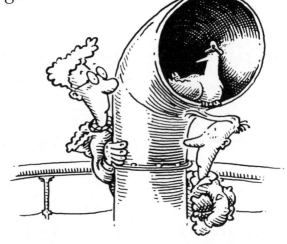

'Great idea,' I said, taking the mickey. 'Or, better still, let's disguise ourselves as a pair of seagulls and perch up there on the mast.'

Then I spotted them. The lifeboats. 'Quick, let's climb into one of those, they'll never look in there – not unless we run into icebergs anyway.' So in we climbed, and no sooner had we covered ourselves with the tarpaulin than there was a great shuddering and the whole ship seemed to turn round on itself. We were off! Soon we'd be digging for diamonds in the Brazilian jungle or building sandcastles on a tropical island. But we had to be patient, we knew that. Those places are a long way away, it could take days, even months.

So we were patient. Very patient. Until after what seemed like hours and hours we decided to eat our rations, which I divided up equally. I gave Midge all the rum and I had all the biscuits. Looking back on it now, that probably wasn't a good idea, especially for Midge.

 What with the rolling of the ship, and not having

had any breakfast, and the excitement, and a couple

of swigs of rum — well you can guess what happened —

woooorrppp! All over the place. We pulled back the sheet and decided to give ourselves up. We were too far away at sea now for the captain to turn back. The worst he could do was to clap us in irons or shiver our timbers.

We climbed down on to the deck and as Midge staggered to the nearest rail to feed the fishes, I looked out to sea hoping to catch sight of a whale, a shoal of dolphins, perhaps see the coast of America coming in to view. And what did I see? The Liver Buildings.

Anyone can make a mistake can't they? I mean, we weren't to know we'd stowed away on a ferryboat.

One that goes from Liverpool to Birkenhead

and back again, toing and froing across the Mersey. We'd done four trips hidden in the

lifeboat and ended up back in Liverpool.
And we'd only been away about an hour
and a half. 'Ah well, so much for running
away to sea,' we thought as we disembarked
(although disembowelled might be a better
word as far as Midge was concerned).
Rum? Yuck.

We got the bus home. My mum and dad
were having their breakfast. 'Aye, aye,' said
my dad, 'here comes the early bird. And what
have you been up to then?'

'I ran away to sea,' I said.

'Mm, that's nice,' said my mum, shaking
out the cornflakes. 'That's nice.'

Big Sisters

Midge's big sister was called Deirdre. She was a girl. Not only was she a girl but she was older than Midge by about a hundred years. Her hobbies were dancing, looking at herself in the mirror and bossing little boys around. Midge's biggest regret in life was that he hadn't been born an only child.

At the end of the summer holidays, the week before we were due back at school, Midge's gran went to stay with her brother in London for a few days, leaving Deirdre in charge. Midge asked if I could stay and keep him company and everyone agreed. (Even Deirdre, surprisingly, although I suppose she reckoned that two heads were easier to hit than one.)

It was good fun at first because we had the house to ourselves, Deirdre being out with her friends all day long, practising being a teenager. Midge and I had our mates around to play cricket in the garden or to play cards in the shed. We had fish and chips twice a day and drank Tizer till the bubbles popped out of our ears.

We stayed up late every night, too, because Deirdre didn't come home until all hours. Out dancing or playing Beauty Queens with her daft pals.

The day before Gran was due home it all changed. We knew something was wrong when Deirdre got up early and started tidying up the house. And singing at the same time (if you could call it singing, more like the

sound of a lorry full of budgies, skidding on a wet road). And not only that, but when we eventually got out of bed she gave us a Mars bar each to help her. In the afternoon, the plot,

like the tomato soup we had for lunch,
thickened, when four of her friends arrived,
loaded down with bottles of cider, sliced
bread, crisps, meat pies, cream crackers and
big hunks of cheese.

'Ooh goody, we're having a party,' said
Midge excitedly. 'How many mates can we
invite?'

The girls stopped buttering the cream
crackers and looked at Deirdre.

(It was so quiet, you could hear a sausage roll.)

'Party? Oh no, we're not having a party . . . we're just . . . we're just . . . having a special tea for Joan's birthday. Aren't we, girls?' The girls nodded and carried on plastering the crackers.

24

'Can we come?' I asked.

'No you can't, it's girls only.' (At this, her friends collapsed into fits of giggles. Sniggerly lot.) 'And besides, I thought it might be a good idea if you and Midge stayed at your house tonight. Just for a change.'

'But I always stay at my house,' I pointed out.

'I mean a change for Midge, you dumb-bell.'

'We'd rather stay here,' said Midge, 'and see the fun.'

'Listen you,' said Deirdre, brandishing the bread knife, 'get one thing straight, I'm just having a little tea party this evening for my girl friends and I don't want you here.' She softened suddenly, like a cobra with a toy mouse. 'Look, here's a pound, if you leave now you can both go to the cinema and then go and stay the night at your friend's. See you tomorrow. Bye.'

With that, Deirdre turned back to her smirking pals and they all carried on talking flibberty-gibberish.

Special tea indeed! It would be a very special tea if it was made out of cider! They were making enough sandwich-spread sandwiches to feed an army. And Midge and I knew where the army would be coming from, Toll Cross Secondary Boys School.

27

So without another word, we packed our pyjamas and toothbrushes into our holdalls, waved a cheery goodbye and set off for the cinema. As if.

Instead, we went to 'Charlie's Cheery Chippy' for our supper and then doubled back to Midge's.

First of all we dumped our holdalls in the shed and then, like a couple of deadly secret agents, let ourselves in through the back door and tiptoed up the stairs. As we suspected, the girls were all in the bathroom, wearing

out the mirror.

We hardly recognized Midge's room when we saw it, because it looked like a second-hand clothes shop. My sleeping bag had been rolled up and put on top of the wardrobe, and his bed was covered with girls' coats.

Just as we were wondering whether to turn them all inside-out and tie the arms together, or merely chuck them all out of the window, the dreaded sound of giggles came hobbling down the landing towards us.

We immediately did what any highly-trained, deadly secret agent would have done in the circumstances ... hid under the bed.

29

Sure enough, in came Deirdre with two of her lieutenants.

'They'll start to arrive any minute now, so Pat, you show them up here to leave their coats, and Maureen, you see to the drinks when they come down.'

The one called Pat (who was a cross between a schoolgirl and a fork-lift truck) moved towards us and plonked herself on the bed. The mattress buckled with pain.

Another six inches to the left and my face would have been ground into the carpet. As it was, we were getting very squashed and uncomfortable.

'They're late aren't they?' said Pat.

'Lads always arrive late at parties,' explained Deirdre, 'it makes them feel grown-up.'

Pat continued: 'And Midge and thingy won't try and spoil everything by coming round will they?'

Thingy looked at Midge, and Midge looked at Thingy. We both tried not to laugh.

31

'They'd better not,' said Deirdre, 'but just
in case they do try to sneak in and spy
on us, I'll lock this door.'

Again, Midge and I looked at each other,
this time not trying not to laugh. Before we
could think of an amazing plan of escape the
front door bell rang. The girls shrieked, and
Pat jumped off the bed twanging the springs.
Six little feet ran to and fro across the room
like clockwork mice, before disappearing out
through the door.

'Quick, now's our chance,' said Midge. I
slid out from under the bed with Midge right
behind me, but was only halfway across the
room when the sound of heavy footsteps on
the stairs warned us that it was too late. There
was nothing we could do except wheel around
on all of our fours and squeeze once more
beneath the bed.

Pat led in four pairs of lads' shoes and then disappeared again to answer the door. Three more pairs shuffled in, followed shortly after by another two. Once they were all together, the owners of the shoes acted all weird, not like lads do normally. They either whispered nervously or talked over-loudly (nervously).

In our heads, Midge and I put pictures to the sounds we could hear: combs pulled through disobedient hair, dandruff patted off shoulders, ties straightened, socks pulled up,

noses blown.

They were as bad as girls the way they fussed over their appearance. Midge and I almost blushed with shame.

Eventually when there was nothing left to squeeze, straighten or blow, they began to drift out, full of pretend bravado. When the last one had gone, and Midge and I were beginning to wonder if we had a chance of escape after all, the door opened, the light was switched off, the door banged shut, and the sound of a key turning in the lock put a karate chop to our hopes.

I don't know if the party was a great success or not. I don't know whether they played hide-and-seek, scrabble, postman's knock or five-a-side football.

I don't know who ate most of the sandwiches (Fork-lift Pat probably), or who drank most of the cider (the same one responsible for the brown stain behind the settee I suppose).

They certainly played records though. Late into the night, the rhythmic thud of rock'n'roll banged on the ceiling like an angry neighbour.

But despite the noise, and despite the discomfort of lying on a hard floor under a bed piled high with coats, Midge and I fell asleep. That's all we could do really: even heroes shrug their shoulders and give up sometimes. Funnily enough, we slept like logs,

too, because neither of us heard people coming into the room and getting their coats, and shouting goodnight, and so forth. The first thing we knew was that it was morning and we were lying under Midge's bed with all our clothes on.

Slowly the enormity of our crime loomed over us like the smothering shadow of the bed.

'What do we do now?' I whispered.

'Sneak downstairs and out, and then come back in again as if we'd stayed the night at yours.'

We both reckoned that Deirdre would be fast asleep, but we took no chances as we crept downstairs and out of the back door as carefully as a couple of cartoon cats.

Around the houses we ran and then let ourselves in at the front door, full of the noisy joys of morning. Once inside though, we were in for a surprise. There were no signs at all of there ever having been a party. The place was as spick as Gran could have wished for. All the cleaning must have been done the night before, or at the crack of dawn. It was as if we had dreamed the whole thing up.

Over cornflakes, Midge and I were chatting on about how sly and efficient big girls could be when the back door slammed open, and in marched Deirdre carrying our holdalls.

'And what time is this to be coming home?' she demanded.

Midge and I lowered our spoons.

'Out all night at your age, it's disgusting.'

'We haven't been anywhere . . .' we protested feebly. 'We stayed at . . .' Before the fibs could arrange themselves, Deirdre's eyes looked into mine.

'Guess who I have just bumped into in the street? Your mother. And she asked if you were enjoying your stay here, and behaving yourself, and why not bring Midge home for the weekend.'

In my mouth, the milk turned sour.

'I know what happened last night,' she continued, 'you can't fool me. You both tried to run away to sea again didn't you?'

'No we didn't ...
No ... we ... er ...
no ... er ... er ...'
We began slowly to
realize that the truth
might sound even worse.

'Just wait until Gran hears about this.' She turned back to me: 'And your father, he'll give you the hiding of your life.'

'But ...'

But ...

But ... But ...

But ... But ... But ...

Midge and I produced a string of buts, but Deirdre butted in again. 'Unless of course ... unless of course' (out of her pocket she produced a toy mouse) '... we can come to some arrangement.'

41

And so, of course, we came to some arrangement. We never mentioned the party to Gran (or anybody else for that matter) and Deirdre said nothing about our running away to sea again. (I know that we hadn't but it seemed easier to let Deirdre think that we had. Or did she?) Maybe she even knew the truth all along. Maybe she had locked the bedroom door on purpose, knowing that we were hiding under the bed.

You can never tell with girls, especially big sisters.

Naming the Dog

One day was just like any other day. And the next wasn't. One day I got up, had my breakfast, went to school, came home, had my tea, went out to play with Midge, came home and went to bed.

The next day was almost exactly the same until I came home from school, and there in the kitchen was a quivering lump of a little thing. A bundle of black and white hair with a stubby tail at one end and a shiny black nose at the other.

You've guessed. It wasn't a hippopotamus or an elephant. It wasn't a snake or a baby giraffe. (It wasn't even a kitten.) It was a dog.

Dog. D–O–G spells what I have been trying to describe.

It must have been love at first sight, because as soon as I walked into the kitchen, he opened his eyes, waggled to his feet and trotted over towards me. I was so surprised I just stood

there open-mouthed. He looked up at me wagging his tail as if he had been waiting for me all his life. If I'd had a tail I would have wagged it as well. Instead, I picked him up and hugged him and ran

44

into the living-room where we rolled around on the carpet and chased each other and played puppy games until Dad made me sit down for tea.

It turned out that a dog belonging to a friend of my dad's had just had puppies; and even though it wasn't Christmas, or within shouting distance of my birthday, Dad had chosen one of the litter as a present for me. (That's a silly word to describe new-born puppies isn't it? Litter. It makes them sound like rubbish. Imagine the adverts: 'Keep Britain Tidy — Take your puppies home with you.' 'Penalty for dropping puppies £25', and so on.)

After tea of course, I didn't call on Midge
but spent the evening with my new four-
legged mate, wrestling and chasing and tug-
of-warring. That night I dreamed
exciting doggy-dreams
starring 'Me and My Dog'.

In one of them, I was shipwrecked and
saved from drowning by My Dog who took
me by the collar and swam to a desert island.

In another, My Dog leaped through the
window of a burning house and dragged me
to safety. In another, Me and My Dog chased
and caught a gang of bank robbers. It was all
very life-like and exhausting. As you can
imagine, when I got out of bed in the morning
I was dog tired.

(That's another funny saying isn't it? Because all the dogs I know are very lively. They are never too tired to go for a run or chase cats, even old dogs who should know better.)

Mrs Fowler overheard me telling Midge all about him during Art and she made me stand up in front of the class and tell everybody.

Usually I hate doing things like that, but for once I quite enjoyed myself because everyone was interested (even Sandra Stewart who thinks she's ever so clever, and she isn't. Well she is, but she's hopeless at football).

When it was discovered that I hadn't as yet given the dog a name, Mrs Fowler became quite excited, and for the remainder of the afternoon all the class had to draw My Dog and describe him in their own words. For homework we all had to think up a good name for him.

Four o'clock couldn't come quick enough. But eventually it did, just like it always does, dragging its feet. Midge and I, eager for doggy larks, raced home so fast, we left the wind standing at the school gates.

When we got to our house there was nobody in, but I had my own key so I opened the front door, half-hoping, half-expecting to be jumped up at and barked at. But no. Not a welcoming yelp. Nothing.

'Here boy,' I called. No reply. We went in.
He wasn't in the kitchen or the living-room.
'I hope he hasn't sneaked upstairs into one of
the bedrooms,' I said. 'Dad warned him about
that.'

'That's probably where he is,' said Midge,
not very convincingly. But he wasn't.

'Maybe your mum's taken him out for a
walk,' said Midge.

'She's at work this afternoon,' I said, trying
to make my voice sound normal even though
my stomach was reaching up and trying to
grab it.

When we went back into the kitchen to search for clues, we saw that the window was open. 'That's funny,' I said, 'no one ever leaves the window open.' A horrible thought put its hands around my throat: 'A burglar must have broken in and stolen him.'

'Burglars don't just steal dogs,' said Midge.

'Dog burglars do,' I said. 'You've heard of cat burglars, so there must be dog burglars too.'

'Let's take a look outside anyway,' said Midge, 'in case he's climbed out and got himself lost.'

We searched the yard and the garden (that didn't take long) as well as those belonging to our next-door neighbours. No luck. So we decided to widen our search, and just as we turned into Beach Road we met three boys from our class.

'What we've got to do,' said Nick (a big blond boy, bossy as boots, whose ambition was to be a sheriff when he grew up), 'is to form a posse. Round up as many kids as possible and scout around the neighbourhood. Everyone split up and tell another kid, and they've got to tell somebody else, and so on, until all the kids in the area are out on the streets searching.' Nick turned to me and put his right hand firmly on my shoulder (the way heroes do in cowboy films) and looked me straight in the eye (I could almost hear western music swelling in the background).

'Don't worry, we'll get your dawg back for you, if it's the last thing we do.' He then turned and galloped down Beach Road into the sunset.

Knowing that we now had others to help search the streets, Midge and I decided to start back at the house and work outwards. (Also, glasses of milk and jam butties were needed to build up our stamina.)

In the next paragraph Midge and I were back in the kitchen thoughtfully munching

when we heard a strange noise. At first, I thought it was coming from Midge's tummy, but it wasn't. It was like a whimper wrapped in tin foil.

A dog sound it certainly was, and a dog in need of help. Before you could say 'Up in a flash' Midge and I were up in a flash and searching everywhere. In the cupboards,

under the oven; in the oven, under the
cupboards; in the fridge, under the sink.

Nothing.

We stopped rushing around and listened.
It came again. A faint plaintive cry that you
heard with the heart not the ear. There was
no doubt about it, the noise was coming from
outside. Midge and I opened the back door
and stepped out. This time we didn't rush
about again in a state of blundering panic, we
simply stood still and listened. For a few

minutes, silence except for the sound of our own breathing, and then it came again. Midge and I looked at each other wide-eyed, and then at the coal bunker beneath the kitchen window. What we called the coal bunker was a heavy wooden box (about the size of a small fridge) with a sloping lid. I opened it, and

there, black as the coal on which he lay, forlorn and shivering, was 'Bunker'.

I lifted him out and hugged him and hugged him. Then Midge hugged him, and we all hugged each other until we were all black with coal dust. That's when Mum and Dad arrived home.

One hour and twenty-four gallons of hot water later, we were all in the living-room discussing the afternoon's adventure. It turned out that Mum was the culprit who had left the kitchen window open, and Dad owned up to not closing the lid of the coal bunker the night before.

Obviously, at some point during the day, the puppy, keen on exploring the outside world, had climbed first on to a chair, then on to the kitchen table, on to the bread bin, out through the open window and either slipped, or jumped into the bunker causing the lid to

bang shut. It must have been a terrible couple
of hours trapped in the dark, but looking at
him as he chased around the room after my
Dad's slipper, he seemed none the worse for
his experience. (To be honest, I think animals'
memories only stretch as far back as their last
meal.)

First thing next morning, Mrs Fowler had me out again in front of the class telling the story. At the end of it everyone clapped and went 'Ah' (even Sandra Stewart, who isn't a bad footballer really).

Then, one by one, they had to call out the name they had chosen. 'Bonzo', 'Scamp', 'Rover', 'Mac' and so on, and so forth. When everybody had finished I told them that the little dog had already chosen its own name. And when I told them what it was, they all agreed that there could be no other.

'Bunker', not a very doggy name we had to admit. But it fitted somehow. And it still does.

Viking Treasure

One Thursday morning, straight after
Assembly, the school was raided by Vikings.
Fierce men with red beards, waving heavy
swords and axes, suddenly emerged from the
back of the hall, and ran between the rows of
innocent children, yelling and clanking. Of
course, they didn't fool me for a minute. Real
Viking warriors, I knew, wouldn't wear false
beards (or, worse still, be seen dead in yellow
and blue trainers). But they were convincing
enough to make most of the kids scream and

get excited, until the headmaster quietened everybody down and introduced the theatre group. (Two of the fiercest-looking warriors, by the way, turned out to be girls, which just goes to show what a big helmet and a blood-stained axe   can do for you.)

They all said hello, and told us that they were touring the schools on Merseyside performing a play about life in Liverpool when the Vikings arrived, thousands of years ago. It was really interesting to learn, not only about the Viking invaders but about the Anglo-Saxons who had lived in the area and the Romans who came later to set up their garrisons. I looked with new eyes at the kids around me and could imagine them as the children of Saxon farmers or Roman soldiers

and suddenly they all seemed more interesting.

That Thursday morning was one of the best times I ever had in school, and made ordinary lessons seem boring. Midge agreed, although what really excited him was the thought of being an actor. What he intended to do when he grew up, he said, was to be a member of a theatre group which visited schools and chased children with large swords. I had to agree that to be an adult and get paid for dressing-up and playing soldiers seemed as good a job as there was.

A week later came half-term. It was
October, and a bullying one. It wore a grey
frown and kicked the leaves about. It shook
the trees and it banged on the window-panes.
But it was mainly bravado. (The real tough
guys, Jan and Feb, could be really mean when
they wanted to. No sooner is Christmas over
than they are holed up in the sky like besieged
gangsters, armed with snow bullets and winds
tipped with ice.)

October may be loud-mouthed, but it's usually dry. So Midge and I were able to go out every day, either playing footy in the park, with other lads who lived nearby, or taking Bunker for long runs along the canal bank.

The days sped by happily enough, but on Friday we felt like doing something different, and Midge had the idea of getting the train out to Formby and then walking back along the shore.

'What we need before we go back to school,' he said, 'is buckets full of sea air.'

So, at about ten o'clock, we set off, our rucksacks stacked with corned-beef sandwiches, dog biscuits and pop; and an hour later we were heading into the hilly sand dunes that range along the shore north from Liverpool. Once you cross through the dunes you come to the flat beach that stretches out to the Irish Sea. Miles and miles of nothing but miles and miles. The hills of sand seemed to offer more fun. So, first things first: we sat on the tough grass on the highest dune we could find and ate our sarnies and drank our pop. (Bunker was too interested in chasing seagulls, so we saved his lunch for later.)

In summer, the place would have been chock-a-block with day-trippers and smooching couples, but that day, thanks to sullen October, we had the battlefield to ourselves.

At first, we were Viking raiders making mincemeat out of the Ancient Brits. Then, we were commandos, sneaking up on enemy soldiers and throwing grenades into their dugouts. Or charging down the sandy slopes, machine-guns blazing. Finally, when we had exhausted ourselves wiping out the German SS, two Roman legions, the entire Sioux nation and countless invaders from outer space, the three brave warriors (well two and a half really) headed down on to the shore and in the direction of home.

Ahead, in the far distance, we could see the twinkling lights, the giant cranes, and tower blocks of Liverpool. And above the city, a cloud of grey smoke hovered, like a bad mood.

Across the river on the opposite side was Birkenhead, and pencilled faintly in behind, were the mountains of Wales.

But when we stopped to look straight out across the bottle-grey waters, where the River Mersey runs into the Irish Sea, no land could be seen. Only ships returning wearily to port, or setting out, spirits high, to see the world.

'Why don't we run away to sea again Midge, and this time do it properly?'

Midge shook his head. 'Nah. I'm going to be an actor, then if I feel like going to sea I can get a part as a sailor in a film. That way you don't get seasick either.'

'Oh, but it's not the same,' I argued.

But Midge wouldn't have it.

'Anyway, you couldn't run away to sea now,' he said, stooping to pick up a small piece of wood.

'Why not?' I asked. Instead of saying anything, Midge threw the stick out into the waves that rolled noisily on to the sand.

The answer to my question bounded joyfully in to fetch it. Of course, Bunker. I could hardly leave him. Mum and Dad would understand my going off in search of adventure — well, at least I hope they would — but not Bunker. There are some things you just can't explain to dogs.

In silence then we walked, and quickly, because we were tired and hungry, and home seemed a long way off.

Only Bunker was tireless as he streaked across the sand in all directions, flapping like a piece of black and white wind.

And it was Bunker of course who found the buried treasure.

He was sniffing around what looked like a small, black pyramid, and barking with an excitement that made us break into a run. As we drew nearer, we could see that it was a box, half buried in the sand. Having dumped it, the waves, now bored, were pulling away and going home to bed.

Needless to say, any thoughts we'd had of going home were now forgotten, as we scooped out the wet sand, and dug and tugged with the superhuman energy we saved for special occasions. Soon we were able to pull it free and look closely at our prize. It was a box of black, rusted metal, about the size of the chest that Long John Silver and the pirates fought over on Treasure Island.

For this was surely gold that had once belonged to Vikings, so vivid were our memories of their school visit the week before. Perhaps, after a raid on Liverpool, one of their ships, laden with stolen treasure, had been wrecked by a storm, and now, hundreds of years later, the sea was giving away one of its dark secrets.

Midge and I dragged the box up the beach and away from the sea's clutches. We couldn't wait to open it and run our fingers through the heavy, gold coins, and try on the priceless crowns ... To fling sapphires and rubies into the darkening air. Diamonds that would out-twinkle even the stars that were beginning to take root in the sky.

The trouble was, we couldn't get it open.
There was no lock, but the lid was firmly
sealed, and try as we might

(we tried for ages)

we couldn't prise it open even a fraction of a
fraction of an inch. Of course, we didn't have
the proper tools. What we were using were
bricks and pieces of metal and wood that were
lying around.

'A hammer and chisel, that's what we need,' I said.

Midge nodded. 'Either that or a few sticks of dynamite.' Bunker wagged his tail in agreement. (I suppose he thought the box would be full of Dog Treasure like juicy bones, crunchy biscuits and huge hunks of meat. As if.)

'Well, we're not going to be able to drag this all the way home,' said Midge, 'and we won't be able to come back tonight with a hammer and chisel. So what do we do?'

'What we do,' I said, 'is bury the box for now and then come back tomorrow with the proper tools.'

Midge agreed. 'But let's be careful where we bury it, so that we can find it again.' We decided it would be safer to bury it in among the sand dunes and away from the beach, where our digging might attract attention.

The box was as heavy and awkward to move as a dead camel, and as the handles were stuck fast, we had to push, shove and drag it up and down the hills of shifting sand, until at last we lay panting, in what seemed like the ideal hiding place. It was a deep hollow, so secret and safe that no one would stumble across it in a million years. Except us of course. And to make sure that we could, Midge and I climbed the highest hill that overlooked it,

and with our backs to the sea, took our bearings. It was almost dark now, but we could still make out a clump of pine trees to the left, a long, low building straight ahead (that seemed part of an airfield), and to the right, an unfastened necklace of bright yellow lamps that curved above a road and dwindled into the distance.

We dug a hole about two foot deep, heaved in the box and covered it with sand. To mark

the spot exactly, we made the letter X, using sticks, bricks, and the leftovers of summer's litter.

'X marks the spot,' said Midge when at last we had finished. 'Goodnight sweet treasure, see you in the morning.'

Then off we set for home. It was cold now, and dark as a shadow's shadow. But we hardly noticed. We were rich, we were famous. No more going out to work for Mum and Dad. No more bus passes for Midge's gran. For Bunker, a fairy-tale kennel, with a lamp-post in every room and a bone-shaped swimming pool in the garden. We would buy ships to stowaway in, schools to play truant from.

In next to no time (which is no time at all) we were home.

Saturday did not turn out as planned. We had both got home so late the night before that the grown-ups were up the wall. I could always tell when my dad was pretending to be angry. He would put on his shouting voice and I would pretend to be sorry. But this time he was upset, I could tell, so was Mum. And his shouting voice was real because it came from deep inside.

As the treasure was going to be our big surprise, Midge and I couldn't give the real reason for our staying out well after bedtime. I made up a fib about getting lost, said I was sorry for upsetting them (which I was) and then went quietly to bed.

Next day I wasn't allowed out at all. Midge called at around midday, but I told him to keep away and lie low until Sunday when, hopefully, all would be forgiven, if not forgotten. Sure enough it was. And as if to celebrate the fact, the sun came out, bright and bold as brass (as it usually does, the day before you go back to school).

During the night Midge had had a brilliant idea. The brilliant idea was for us to ride out to Formby on our bikes, open the box with a hammer and chisel, and either (a) bring back the booty in our cycle bags, or (b) rest the box (if we failed to open it) between the crossbars of both bikes and wheel it home. Brilliant.

As Bunker didn't have a bike
to ride, he had to stay behind
as Midge and I pedalled
forth on our great adventure.
It was a pleasant ride on the
coast road that runs to Southport,
with a fresh wind behind, pushing us along.
Impatiently almost.

In no time at all (which is next to no time),
we turned left off the main road, through
Formby village, past the railway station and
on to the track that leads down into the sandy

hills. The going quickly became heavy, and the only way we could manage was to shoulder our bikes and stagger up and down the dunes until we reached the firmer sand near the sea. There we remounted and cycled slowly along in search of the spot where Bunker had first discovered the box.

We half hoped that the footprints we had left on Friday would still be waiting for us, eager to show us the way. But no such luck. The sea, the old sneak-thief, had nipped in overnight and taken them. (As I cycled, I wondered what the sea did with all those footprints, stolen from the shore. On the ocean floor somewhere, are they all neatly piled up waiting for their owners to come and collect them?)

We stopped when we thought we recognized the part of the beach where the box had been washed up, and turned left into the sand dunes. Following what we hoped was the path we had taken. Once more, we humped the bikes on to our shoulders and staggered up and down the hills in search of the spot marked X.

Being a Sunday afternoon, and sunny into the bargain, there were quite a few people about: joggers, dog walkers, lads playing football. They must have thought us very odd.

After ten minutes of slithering and sliding, we collapsed into two tangled heaps. 'Whose brilliant idea was it to bring the bikes?' I said. Midge looked glum.

'They're slowing us down too much, and we can't leave them anywhere in case they get pinched.'

Midge shook some sand out of his ear and said nothing. Then his face lit up: 'I've got a brilliant idea. Why don't we bury the bikes here, mark the spot with an X, and then when we've found the box, come back and dig them up. Brilliant.' I looked at him to see if he was being serious.

'Are you being serious?' I asked. His face broke into a grin. The idea of our spending hours and hours and hours searching for buried bikes was so crazy that I jumped on him and tried to push his face into the sand, but couldn't for laughing. We rolled around then, fighting and giggling until at last we lay on our backs, dizzy and panting. The sky above spun slowly round and round.

'If only we had a helicopter,' I said, 'we'd find the treasure in a couple of minutes.'

'But we haven't,' said Midge, 'so it's no use thinking about it.'

I sat up. 'Let's start again, but this time we'll

take it in turns. One looks after the bikes while the other searches.'

And that's just what we did. For hours. The one minding the bikes sat on the beach, where he could easily be seen, while the other went inland and did the search. But not only were we unable to find the X, we couldn't even recognize the landmarks we had noted to give us our bearings. There were clumps of pine trees everywhere and lots of low buildings in the distance, with roads running in all directions.

Everything looked so different in the afternoon light. And of course, we couldn't wait until it got dark. Not with all the trouble we had caused on Friday. So, with heavy hearts and heavy shoes (which were full of sand — the shoes, that is, not the hearts), we cycled home.

The ride back was murder. We were now cycling against a wind that seemed determined not to let us get past. Most of the journey was spent in silence, heads down, legs that ached, pumping away.

As we neared Litherland, however, the wind stood aside and let us through. Able to sit upright on our saddles for the first time, and get our breath back, I suggested to Midge that we should tell the grown-ups about the treasure. We were back at school the next day, so it was important that they were let into the secret. My dad could organize a proper search party, using friends from work. He might even be able to fly a helicopter. Midge agreed that under the circumstances it made good sense. And so, as soon as we got back to ours, we told Mum and Dad the whole story.

When we had finished telling them, we probably thought that Dad would smile proudly and shake our hands, and that Mum would hug and kiss us, tears of joy streaming down her cheeks.

'What clever boys!' they would say. 'Discovering Viking treasure, and making us all richer than our wildest dreams. What clever, clever boys!'

But it wasn't like that. Not like that at all.
Mum went pale and Dad began shouting. It
wasn't the sort of shouting that came from
deep inside. It was the sort that he put on
when he wanted you to pay attention. The
shouting didn't last long, but the lecture that
followed it did. It was all about poisons and
chemicals and explosives. And about how,
when he was a boy, one of his friends had had
his hand blown off when opening a box found
on the beach. There are horrible accidents,
even worse than that, every year, he said.

When he had finished, Midge and I were paler than Mum. Then Midge had another of his 'brilliant' ideas: 'Maybe if we told the police, we might get a reward.'

For the first time that evening, Dad smiled. 'There wouldn't be any reward, I'm afraid, but you could report it to the police. The problem would be finding it. You see, those sand dunes may look like miniature mountains but they're not. They are made out of sand and they shift and move whenever the wind blows. The X that you made will have vanished forever. And the box? Well it may turn up again one day. And if it does, let's hope that whoever finds it has got more sense than you two. Viking treasure indeed!'

The next day was school again as usual, and we heard no more about the box after that. There was nothing on television about explosions on Formby beach. No reports of Viking treasure being discovered. It must be buried still beneath the sand. That box of dark secrets, impatient to be opened.